Praises for

Finding Love in First Corinthirns Thirteen

As believers, love is a compelling phenomenon in our walk and relationship with the Lord. As loaded as it is, the choice of love as a subject for this book makes it a must-read for everyone. The author systematically expounds upon the need to go beyond regarding love as a theoretical concept. She emphasizes the imperative for us to listen to our Lord's commandment. We must see love as an action word worthy of practice amongst ourselves in our daily lives in our homes, churches, workplaces, schools, market places, etc.

—Pastor Tochi

***

When we listen to the Lord's injunction, we are in obedience. When we listen not, we are in disobedience. The author dutifully points out God's immutable style of rewarding compliance and the inescapable consequences of disobedience. The word of God in Isaiah 1:19-20 anchors her point. "If you are willing and obedient, you shall eat the good of the land, but if you refuse and rebel, you shall be devoured by the sword for the mouth of the Lord hath spoken it."

In agreement with the author, love, among many other factors, is the uniqueness of our oneness as God's creation.

—Hans C.

***

Reviews for 1Cor.13

I loved the flow of this book, and you can sense that this book is Spirit-filled from the beginning to the end. The anointing is so powerful, and it is evident that the author is gifted. We need more Spirit-filled books and authors like this woman to give us God's perspective and not man's.

—Regina C

***

Let me start by saying that this is one of the best Christian books that I have read in a long time. I had to read it repeatedly to allow each verse to absorb in my spirit. God's love is assuring, and it is demonstrated in this book. There is no doubt that God is still speaking to us through His servants today.

—Kaleb W

***

More grace to this author and I am definitely a fan now because I can't wait to read more books written by her.

—John E

FINDING LOVE IN FIRST CORINTHIANS THIRTEEN

HELEN CLEMENT

Published by KHARIS PUBLISHING, imprint of KHARIS MEDIA LLC.

Copyright © 2022 Helen Clement

ISBN-13: 978-1-63746-109-9

ISBN-10: 1-63746-109-7

Library of Congress Control Number: 2022931595

All KHARIS PUBLISHING products are available at special quantity discounts for bulk purchase for sales promotions, premiums, fund-raising, and educational needs. For details, contact:

Kharis Media LLC
Tel: 1-479-599-8657
support@kharispublishing.com
www.kharispublishing.com

DEDICATIONS

My sweetest love, God the Holy Spirit.
Maya G. with love and
To all of God's children in the world.

INTRODUCTION

I started writing the verses in First Corinthians Chapter Thirteen on December 16, 2020 and finished on February 13, 2021. I had approximately nine-thousand-word counts. I went back to the Lord on September 3, 2021, to add and expand more to His words in each verse to bring the word counts to at least twenty thousand. I finally completed writing these beautiful messages in this book on November 5, 2021. What a tremendous blessing this virtue truly is. Love is everything.

Love is priceless beloved, and it is the gift that only God can give us for complete happiness. We cannot buy it, and only God's love endures daily from generation to generation. God's love is not like the love that the world has. It is this divine love that fills and sustains our souls every day. We cannot have this love or understand this love without getting to know the One who can love us unconditionally and absolutely. Love is the life that we have and the heart in our hearts, and it is vital to differentiate God's love from the sensual love that the world so desires.

Love is the virtue that carries us higher in this spiritual plane through faith when we are willing to learn of God. We must be filled with love because it is the greatest essence of who God is and one of the reasons why we are alive today. Let us thank the Son for the love that He has demonstrated on the cross for us because there is no greater expression of love to humankind than the One Jesus Christ; the Son demonstrated in Calvary on the cross. Let us love like this. Let us embrace one another even with our differences because that is what makes us unique. You see, God is a multi-diverse God who has made us in His image and likeness and extraordinary people and individual with diverse talents that we are.

Let us thank God for His love that keeps shinning His glory in our lives. Let us love others and resist and desist from judging one another because if we are judged, we would not have the footing to stand upon. "Through the Lord's mercy, we are not consumed, Because His compassion fails not, they are new every morning; Great is Your faithfulness" (Lm.3:22–23). Love one another. Show others that you care not only by words but through actions. The most incredible show of love is not demonstrated by talks but by actions, and we do not need to announce to the world what we do for others. God is the love that radiates in our souls, and in turn, we let that beaming lights of love shine so that others can see that the One who is living in us is worthy of all praise.

Love is the key to the meaning of life. It is the whole life that we are given in the Son and the life that cannot be taken for granted. Love moves us to do for others, and it is an action word. Love is not passive. Love is forgiveness and every good thing that we can imagine. The essence of God is love, and that is why we must love our neighbors as we love ourselves (Mt.22:37–39). We can-not claim to love God and hate our fellow man. "If someone says, "I love God," and hates his brother, he is a liar; for he who does not love his brother whom he has seen, how can he love God whom he has not seen?" (1Jn.4:20). God is the love that radiates through us.

We cannot say we belong to God and walk in hate. That is contrary to God's word. Haters are destined to perish if they do not repent from their hatred of others. Haters are doomed, and the life that awaits them is hell. Love shines in our souls and shows others that we are indeed the children of God. Beloved, love is the engine that powers our spiritual gifts from God. Love moves everything. We must have enough love to push the im-movable. Love is why many cannot move forward and be successful in all they do. They are loaded in their hearts with bitterness that leads to hate and a lack of forgiveness. We must let go of these things to move ahead in life. Love combats all the sufferings in the world.

A little love here and a little love there make the universe an excellent place for all. Love draws us together through one common thread, and that is humanity. Do unto others as you would like them to do unto you (Mt.7:12) is the highest form of mutual respect derived from absolute love. Love is the virtue that brings perfection through the grace of God by faith in the Son.

Love is the essence of our being. It is the heart of the Spirit and the light that shines in our paths daily. It would be a wonderful world if we could just rid it of all the wickedness and replace it with love. Love is the foundation of the kingdom of God and love is the reason we are saved through grace by faith.

Love is the greatest(1Cor.13:13), and we must all desire to walk in love. We must all desire to show love. We must all desire to express kindness. We must all desire to speak a good word to others. We must all desire to love as God has loved us. Judgment comes when true repentance fails. God will judge those who refuse to love others. Remember that "mercy triumphs over judgment" (Jm.2:13), and God's unconditional love keep us in His mercy and goodness daily. Let us love fervently without reservations. Let us express true love towards others. We cannot continue to see others based on what they look like or how they talk, their religions, whom they are married to, their names, or where they come from.

Our business is to love everyone regardless of who they are, and God will oversee the judgment and the condemnation part. Let us be reminded and consider ourselves judged too if we judged others. Moreover, love is the virtue that brings satisfaction to the soul. We must try it out every day. Many ministers cannot move mightily in their offices and spiritual gifts because they do not genuinely express love to others in humility. Until we learn to love and serve in humility, we cannot bring the world to God. We lack in love for others, and righteousness is another reason we cannot draw the world to

God, and until these are reconciled, there will not be any great revival, and many will be spiritually dead.

Love is the virtue that gives absolute empowerment and spiritual capabilities through faith. Love is the key to understanding that propels us to the most incredible heights in ministry. Many are just dead inside, and they are slow because nothing can sustain them except for this love from God, but they refuse to extend that love to others. Many claim to belong to God, but they are of the devil when looking at their fruits. Their father's work the devil they do, and they do not fool us. We must understand that love is effortless when our hearts are pure towards others. Love is effortless when we live with a pure conscience daily.

You see church leaders practicing and supporting hatred, and do not be fooled because they are not of God. God is love. "And we have known and believed the love that God has for us. God is love, and he who abides in love abides in God, and God in him" (1Jn.4:16). We belong to God. Love is not only the greatest virtue but the virtue that catapults us to higher spiritual under-standing when our attention stays on Christ only. Love is the light of the soul. It is the virtue that heals the soul. Once taken, love is the pill that starts to work imm-ediately on contact. We must practice love. It is a virtue and a fruit that must be cultivated to be empowered by it. Love is the manifestation of priceless life, yet we cannot live without it.

Love moves mightily in all our lives when we open our hearts truly and stop harboring toxins inside. Love is the essential virtue apart from faith, obedience, righteousness, and holiness of navigating the spiritual realm. We still have not gotten it when it comes to this virtue. We still have a long way to go to hold onto this life that God has given to us. There are so many manifestations of evil in the world because love has ceased to exist in all our lives. Many hearts are filled with wickedness. Many hearts are evil. Many hearts are hard. Many hearts are unrepentant. Many hearts are filled with jealousy and envy that leads to atrocities.

Beloved, love is the channel by which we can be made whole body, soul, and spirit. We must practice love to live freely in peace. We must learn to extend this eternal love that radiates from God to us to others. Hate kills the life that we have been blessed with. Wickedness is the reason you see many nations in bondage. Beloved, we must come to God and repent from our evil ways. Love is the only avenue that we can do this in Christ. Love is the air that we breathe daily. Love is the life we have been given to and take for granted every day. Love is all and conquers everything.

TABLE OF CONTENTS

VERSE ONE

⋘❦⋙

LOVE IS THE ENGINE THAT POWERS MINISTRIES.

Though I speak with the tongues of men and angels but have not love, I have become sounding brass or a clanging cymbal.

Everything we do in this life hangs only on love. It does not matter how highly gifted and anointed we are; we have become empty vessels without love. Love is the virtue that fulfills us absolutely in our walk with God and humanity. Love is not what we do to make others love us because it is a spirit that God has given to all of humankind to demonstrate the goodness of God in their lives. Through love, we are indeed known as the children of God. Through love, we move mightily in our gifts and offices. We can do our ministries to absolute contentment in Christ Jesus through love. Love is the engine that powers ministries, and it is a vital part of our journey in all that we do for God, either by words or through our actions. Love is the most essential of all the virtues apart from faith that brings God closer to our lives, and we must strive to be filled with this virtue.

We could be all we could be in this world and have every worldly possession, but we are dead without love. Love is the heartbeat of humanity. It is the cord that ties us spiritually to our existence. Love is the fibers in our bodies that give true meaning to our existence. Love cannot fail even when everything else fails. God's love in our lives is constant, and nothing can separate us from this love. (Rm.8:31–39). We must follow God in this regard. We must have love in our hearts for our fellow men regardless of who they are. "Owe nothing to no one except to love them for whoever fulfills that has fulfilled the law" (Rm.13:8). Love is the channel by which we genuinely grow faithfully in the supernatural and the things of God through faith. Love matters, and it is the virtue that sharpens and quickens our spirit man to be in tune with God's through the help of the Holy Spirit.

Love sees no evil. Love does not bear false witness against anyone. Love does not judge anyone. Love does not tell lies. Love is a long-suffering virtue that endures all things. Love does not hold any grudges. It is quick to forgive. It is a virtue that radiates through mercy and kindness. We must understand that love needs to abound in all our lives daily for us to be in the blessed state that God has ordained for all His people on earth. We must represent God daily in this virtue because that is who God truly is; otherwise, how can we stand at all? Love is the virtue that brings goodness. Beloved, we cannot claim to know God and hate our brethren. "But if anyone loves

God, this one is known by Him" (1Cor.8:3). Love is good. Love is the bubbling joy in our souls that shines and radiates the glory of the Son in our lives through the help of the Holy Spirit. No matter how gifted we are, even if we understand all mysteries and speak in the tongues of angels. All of these do not matter or count.

What matters to God is love. Without love, we are dead, just as without faith, we are spiritually dead. Those who do not love and continue to hate will have themselves to blame on the day of judgment. Rest assured that they will be judged as murderers and unbelievers. Their fate will be the same as the unbelievers. Let us live not in words only but through our actions. Love is the vehicle upon which we stand daily through faith in the Son. Speak that language. Have it in abundance. Let others see it. Shine and the glory of God will dwell in your presence forever and ever.

Love is what defines us and sets us apart from the world. Love is the key to obtaining God's ordained blessings in our lives, and many have not yet figured that out, and they are out of touch and living out of God's will. You see the sorrows in the world, and that is not the work of God but what they have brought upon themselves through their act of wickedness. We must return to our first love. We must understand the first and the most important commandment of God. We must embrace this God with everything in our being, and only then can we begin to make headway in all that we choose to do.

The absence of love is detrimental to our soul. It keeps the soul locked in mysteries, and we must end and break the chains to forge ahead in life. Love is the virtue that takes us to the places unimagined through faith in the Son, and that is why we all need to be filled abundantly with it to be blessed. Love is the key to tapping into this great relationship with God through faith, and it is the only key that opens everything along with faith in God's storehouses. Love has many potentials, and it is always waiting to be tapped into to unlock the goody bags that God has for us.

Beloved, we need love in abundance to forge ahead and be victoriously successful in all that God has dispatched to us. Let us be clear that love is all, and no matter how talented and gifted we are, we need the abundance and the flourishing of love to fly higher in this spiritual realm that only God can bequeath to us. Love can move where others cannot, and it is the power engine of all the other virtues. We cannot claim to belong to God without the abundance of this virtue flowing in us and through us.

No matter the gifts we are endowed with, and without love, we will quietly fade away, fade out, fade over, and be gone in a short while. Love is a perfecter and a spirit, and it is always working in us to perfect us to stand in God's presence through this faith in the Son. We must love, and never should we have hate in our hearts. We must express it every day by our actions. We must go the extra mile and extend kindness that shows authentic love.

Love carries us absolutely, and there is no other way to express this clearly in simple terms. Love is everything we have in this life, and it is the best of all gifts that money cannot buy. Love is a commandment from God, and we cannot negotiate our way out of it. It is the final say, and we must love one another as Christ has loved us. Love is the key to true destiny fulfillment, and many are still grappling with it. They think that they can have hate in their hearts towards others and still call on the name of God.

We are told not to be deceived because "God is not mocked; for whatever a man sows, that he will also reap" (Ga.6:7). We must be careful what we sow because it comes back to us one way or the other in ways that we do not expect. We must understand that love has its principles and when we realize that, we are ready to conquer the world. One of the principles of love is in (Rm.13:8), "Owe no one anything except to love one another, for he who loves another has fulfilled the law." Love shines in our souls daily, and it is the beautiful heart that embraces everyone.

Love is a beautiful personality that admires others and gives kind words of encouragement. It is the friendly smile shown towards others that brighten someone else's day. It is the music and the birds that sing every day. It is the peace that God has given to us. It is the blessings that keep us in God's light and favor. Beloved, we cannot say that we are the children of God and be filled with hate. We cannot walk truthfully in this journey and say that

God is our Father when we do things contrary to His words.

We must have the qualities of God as we walk in this journey. We must show others love through our actions and not by what we say. No matter how much we have in the bank, our family connections, or have everything that money could buy, and if we do not love, we become people after briefly observing themselves in a mirror fades away in a brief moment in time. Love is the virtue that brings us this peace and more of God. It is the love of God's heart that lives in our hearts.

Without love, we are incomplete. Without love, we are dead spiritually. Without love, we cannot be who God has made us be. Without love, we are just running empty in this life. Love is the difference that makes life worth living. Love is the spirit that keeps moving us in a higher plane. Love is why we are here on earth because of the great love that the Father of our Lord Jesus Christ has for us. Love is authentic, and there is no way around it. God's commandment is clear. Let us walk in this virtue. Let us live this life filled with love because that is God's expression of love radiating in us. Love is a beautiful thing that God has made unique and given to us.

VERSE TWO

LOVE RADIATES IN ALL OUR LIVES

And though I have the gift of prophecy, and understand all mysteries and all knowledge, and though I have all faith so that I could remove mountains, but have not love, I am nothing.

Without love, we are spiritually dead. Without love, we are nothing. Without love, we cannot operate fully in our gifts to the capacity we ought to. Without love, we cannot be called the children of God. Without love, we are left in limbo. We must learn love. We must practice it daily. We must get to the point where love drives our motivation in this journey and not by anything else. Love is the key to the blessings that are immeasurable that God has poured down upon us through Christ Jesus. Love carries us steadily in this journey. It is the power that works with grace to strengthen and empower us. Love is the driving force behind all that we do for God. Our gifts must give way for love to manifest solely. Love lasts forever, and we cannot say that about every other thing. You see, we must increase in this virtue daily just as in faith to stand before God daily.

Love is the virtue that brings knowledge and the abundance of God's mercy. The fruits of love are unlimited and connected to every other virtue. We cannot separate love from anything or other virtues because they are intertwined. Love is the gift that lasts forever and is a spirit that stays in us from God the Father to us through His Son, Jesus Christ. Love made us who we are in this journey. By it, we stand solid through grace and faith. Love determines our purpose. By it, we can function in our gifts. We must understand that without love, we are nothing, and it does not matter how highly anointed or gifted we are in this ministry. Love is the front, the back, the center, and the theme of this ministry that we have in Christ Jesus. Love is the mother of kindness and long-suffering. Love opens the channel by which we obtain the gifts of the Holy Spirit through faith.

Love stands alone in itself, and it is a mighty force that we all need to move in ministries. Love is the purpose, and until we understand the cause, the purpose dwindles. Beloved, love is the virtue that shines the glory of God in all our lives. It is the beaming lights in our soul and the essence of our being. It is the foundation that is built on solid ground. It is the life that keeps us going and the grace that keeps us in the mercy of Jesus Christ. It does not matter how gifted we are or our faith in this journey; we have become nothing without love.

Without love, we cannot be who we are supposed to be spiritually. We cannot operate in the capacity we are supposed to with our gifts. Many are dead spiritually because they lack the abundance of this virtue. Love must not only be through words but actions. Actions they say speak louder than words. Love is always doing and going above and beyond. Love is always comforting and rejoicing with others. Love is always hopeful, caring, and kind. Love is a generous spirit that stems from the knowledge of who God is to us, and by this knowledge, we are made to stand confidently and not puffed up.

Love is the virtue of encouragement and the truth that brings inner peace to our lives. Love must be demonstrated in all that we do in the world. Show and tell is the opposite of love. We do not do that. Love is everything, and it is not as the world defines it.

Love is the perfect gift that we all should desire with all our hearts. Love is the gift that many lack forging ahead in their ministry. Love is what sustains us after everything else fails. We must have the abundance of this virtue to move in the spiritual realm. No matter how gifted we are and have all knowledge, without love, we are nothing. Without love, we are spiritually incapacitated. Without love, we cannot live the God fully ordained life.

Love is the life that sustains us through this journey, and we cannot begin to stress the importance of this great virtue. We need love to operate in our gifts and offices that God has called us into, but many do not understand that love is the power engine of spiritual gifts.

We must have this virtue that propels us into these beaming lights that shine ever so brightly in the darkness. Let us continue to share love and receive love. We, the Father, the Son, and the Holy Spirit do not mean this sensual love that does not express the agape love that God has infused in us.

Love is the food of the soul, and we must nourish it daily to grow. Love is the music that sings beautifully and increases the joy and gladness in our souls. We need the abundance of this virtue. We must strive to be filled with love. We must give it entirely and show others that we are truly the children of God by our actions. You see, we cannot stress this enough that nothing else remains, but God's love is constant and stays. God's word also abides forever.

The truth is that love will not fade away. God is love, and this is expressed by the way we engage with others through our actions, through what we do and do not do. No matter how gifted or highly anointed we are, we become a figment of our imagination without love. Love is the expression of goodness that keeps surrounding us day by day.

We need love to combat the ills of the world. We need love to heal the wounded spirit. We need love to open the clogged pipes. We need love to live in unity and peace.

Understanding this virtue brings tremendous know-ledge to all since many are still under the enemy's hold.

Love happens to us all, which is why we are still alive today because of God's most wondrous love for humankind. Let us follow in the footsteps of Christ. Let us emulate His mannerisms. Love activates everything, and there is nothing that it cannot do. We must strive to be filled every day with this virtue and walk in love. Love is life, and without it, we are dead spiritually. You see, it does not matter how gifted and talented we are, and without love, we are empty. Love is the goodness that brings forth the glory of the Son to our lives and begins to radiate in all that we do in His name for others. We cannot say that God is our Father and lack in this fruit and virtue because the very essence of our eternal God is love.

Love is what created us and brought us to God through this grace by faith. God's love for us is permanent and cannot diminish or change over time like the love from humankind. We must learn to practice this love until we become perfects at it because we lack in love. The Children of God in the world should demonstrate much love that draws others to God and not isolate them. Their love should be heavenly based that heals, brings hopes, gives assurance, build-up, and encourages. No child of God should have hate in their hearts or let the word hate comes out of their mouth.

We must believe that hatred comes from a place of wickedness and darkness, and no child of God should entangle themselves in these yokes of bondage. Let us be quick to understand and gain the knowledge that makes us free in Christ. Many think that they could live without this agape love that comes from Christ, but unless they have the abundance of God's Spirit in them and walk with Him, they will continue to be used by the devil to execute his wickedness and hatred.

We must speak good words that unite. We must bring harmony to all our lives through the peace of God. We cannot be the servants of God and engage ourselves in divisions, practice separation, disunity, murders, discrimination, racism, and other works of darkness. We must understand the qualities and the characters of God to know that He is love and light. Beloved, walking in spiritual offices or gifts does not make us super and beyond reproach, and love is the key to perfection in all that we do, and it endures forever after everything is gone. Rest in this hope. Believe that love fulfills the law. Make no mistake about it and let the love of God abides in you and express the same love to others. May we abound in this virtue day by day through the help of the Son by the mighty power of the Holy Spirit forever and ever. Amen.

VERSE THREE

LOVE CARRIES US THROUGH MERCY

And though I bestow all my goods to feed the poor, and though I give my body to be burned, but have not love, it profits me nothing.

Beloved, we must be assured that love carries us in this journey through the mercy of God. God is love, and everything about who God is apart from this saving faith is about love. "For God so loved the world that He gave His only begotten Son, that whoever believes in Him should not perish but have everlasting life" (Jn.3:16). That is the true love that binds us to God through faith in the Son. This eternal love radiates in all our lives, and we see it through the grace God blesses us with daily, through this mercy, kindness, goodness, generosity, blessings, long-suffering, and so much more. God continues to demonstrate His love for us even after Christ laid His life on the cross for us and daily (Rm.5:8). We must reciprocate this love and extend it to others.

Through this virtue, we can show the world that we are indeed the children of God and not of the evil one. Through this virtue, we can heal nations and humanity. Through this virtue, we can be united nations under God. Through this virtue, we move and live in the fullness of God, the Father, the Son, and the Holy Spirit. Love carries us through the mercy of this benevolent God, and we should never let go of it no matter what happens. Love is the greatest apart from faith that keeps us closer to God's heart. No matter who we are or our status in this life, we must be filled with love. The greatest commandment in the law is this; "You shall love the Lord your God with all your heart, with all your soul, and with all your mind. And the second is like it: You shall love your neighbor as yourself. On these two commandments hang all the Law and the Prophets" (Mt.22:38–40). Love is everything, and there is no substitute for it. Live love.

Express it by your actions and not through words only. Love is the life we have every day, and we cannot live without it. Rich or poor, and it does not matter the race, the gender, or the nationality, love happens to us all through the kindness of this one God who made all men in His image and His likeness, and this God is Jesus Christ. Without love, we have nothing. It does not matter how rich or how many possessions we possess. Love is the essence of our being. Love is the motivation that keeps us steady in this life's journey. Love is the virtue of hope that brings a better future. Love is the healings in our souls and the forgiveness that lights the blessings of tomorrow. God is love, and we cannot hate and say that we are the children of God. True love is displayed by and from the generosity of our actions, not words. Our actions cause things to take place either for the good of the people or for the bad. Love every day. Move in this virtue abundantly.

We cannot stress the importance of this virtue enough. Love is everything, and in it, we derived the goodness of God all around us and followed us throughout the rest of our days. Believe in whatever you want, but love is crucial to our survival on this earth, and no matter how accomplished or have everything we want, without love, we are just like a boat stranded in the middle of the ocean. Love is the virtue that is needed in all our lives to receive the blessings of God. However, many refuse to walk in it or be filled with it because their hearts are evil. Until they come clean and have pure hearts towards others, they will remain in one spot, and that is not putting a curse on anyone, but that is how this virtue operates.

We must understand spiritual stuff to gain the blessings of spiritual things because knowledge is the key to empowerment. Knowledge is the key to a successful life. Knowledge brings freedom. Knowledge is the aptitude on a higher spiritual plane, and until we gain that, we remain floating on the surface. Let us try love and be filled with it. It does not get any better than love because it is all in one virtue. Love is the fountain of life and from the beginning to the end of life that we have. Let us hold onto it.

We must rest assured that love is a powerful virtue that completes us in and out and makes us into better people as we behold ourselves in a mirror day by day and like what we see. Love is the inner beauty that we must desire more than the outward facade beauty that we cherish. True love lasts for life, which Christ has given to us, and it is our responsibility to express that same kind of love towards others. Love is everything, and through it, we are made perfect by faith through grace. Let us hold onto this love with all our hearts and follow in God's footsteps.

Love is the music that the soul makes, and let us bless the Lord of our lives for filling our souls with joy through the expression of this virtue. We must never let go of life because it is intertwined with love. We gain nothing, and we will be nothing until our lives fully express this love that God has deposited in us through Christ by the power of the Holy Spirit. Love shines beautifully in our souls as the world draws nearer to God because of the beaming lights that they see in us. Do not forget that, and do not forget to show this expression of love every day to everyone we meet.

The critical element of love is that it never fails. It is constant and on the move. It is what we live for in Christ and the life that God has given us to stand solid in trials and tribulations. We cannot fail because that is not an option in this journey. That is why God's love surrounds us, and nothing can ever separate us from this great love that God has for us all (Rm.8:35) even when we misbehave and fall short of His glory day by day. In this love, we rejoice. In this love, we look forward to the blessings of the day. In this love, we are kept in God's mercy.

We must understand this virtue to live the life of Christ. We must emulate the characters of God to forge ahead and be successful in our undertakings. We must have the mind of Christ and act like Him. God is love, and love is a non-negotiable virtue. We must walk in love if we say that God is our Father. We must demonstrate this virtue to be known by the fruits that we bear. God's love radiates in us, and we must show it to others with this same love. "And the King will answer and say to them, 'Assuredly, I say to you, inasmuch as you did it to one of the least of these My brethren, you did it to Me'" (Mt.25:40) is the highest form of love.

Go the extra mile. Show the love of Christ that brings perfect healings to others. Demonstrate by your actions and not by words alone. Never delay kindness and caring. God's gift of love is the best gift that we must all desire to have and to practice. We must practice love and have it in abundance to be nearer to God. Love is essential in this journey and this life. We need love to be made complete. We need love to be who God has made us to be. We can seriously look at many from a distance and see that they do not belong to God because they do not have this virtue.

We cannot say in honesty that we are the children of God and hate and kill one another. We cannot call on God and have no love for His children. We cannot say that we are the children of God when we follow the devil and have the devil's traits in us. We are known by the fruits we display towards others, and the way we treat others shows who our true father is. We must understand that God is love, and we are love too. God is the love that lives forever in our hearts, and we must show this wondrous love of God in our lives towards others.

We must stop judging others because of how they look, what their names are, how they talk, because of their genders, or their race, or their religions or nationality, and the list goes on. When we continue to judge and condemn others, we are effectively condemning and judging ourselves. Let us take our mouths away from others. Let us kill the hate in our hearts with love. You see, love is a priceless virtue. Money cannot buy it; otherwise, the rich folks in the world would have bought it. It is a spirit, and we must be open to the Holy Spirit to have it mightily in our lives.

Love changes us from these ordinary people to these beaming lights that shine ever so brightly in the darkness. Beloved, no matter how talented, rich, or gifted we are, we are like empty shells if we have no love inside. We are like wells without waters. We are like a car without an engine inside. We are lifeless because love is the organ that gives life to everything. Let us move in it. Let us live in it. Let us show others this great love that God has given to us in the Son. Beloved, love is good and to be desired daily. Love is the sweet music in the soul that will not stop playing. Love is the gift of joy and gladness that God infused in us to help us deal with the hurts in the world day by day. Walk in this virtue.

VERSE FOUR

---•◈•---

LOVE IS PLANTED IN PATIENCE

Love suffers long and is kind; love does not envy; love does not parade itself, is not puffed up.

Beloved, love is planted in patience. It is the virtue that endures and bears with others in patience. Love is not a superficial virtue, nor can it be sensual. Love is not lust but the token of God's heart that is emerged in ours. God is love, and we must be like God. God is the Father of all peoples and not just one nation. Love is not proud, nor can it be envy. Love is a perfect virtue that continues to shine this light of God upon our lives daily. Love does not parade itself because it is a virtue that is filled with humility. Humility is the essence of love, and both work alongside each other in ministries. We must be filled with this virtue to move mightily in our gifts and offices.

We must understand that love is the virtue that brings complete healings through patience. Love is a long-suffering virtue, and the fruits of love are joy, peace, kindness, gentleness, goodness, and long-suffering. We must understand that love works along the sides of all the other virtues and cannot be separated from them. Love does not go around judging others. It does not look at the color of our skins. It does not hold grudges. It does not hate. Love is a perfect virtue that we must have in abundance. We must combat the evils in the world with this healing virtue. Love works with faith. They are great partners. Faith and love co-existed in the same spiritual realm of magnitude.

Love, faith, and hope abide forever but loves superseded them in many aspects but not much (1Cor.13:13). Love is the life that Christ gave to us on the cross, and that life still speaks true today in all our lives as we understand the eternal love of God for us. God not only demonstrated this love to us through Christ but filled us with it by faith. Love is a spirit as well as a virtue and a fruit. Many lack this virtue because they are held in bondage and darkness. They are in darkness because they have not opened their hearts to God. As a result, they are entirely led by the devil. Wickedness is embedded in darkness. It is one of the devil's works, but love is light, and God is love and the light of the world. Love is simple because life is simple when we love from our hearts and stop the hating that the enemy uses to divide, steal, kill and destroy (Jn.10:10a) in the world. Love is the virtue that brings peace, unity, and harmony to us, and we must learn to fellowship with God in this love through the help of the Holy Spirit. Love is not puffed up.

Love is a virtue that brings fulfillment, and humility is the channel by which that is done. We must keep asking God, and never should we assume knowing anything without God. We must keep seeking God, and never should we stop looking for God's directions, opinions, and guidance in this journey. We must keep knocking, and never should we think for one second that we can operate outside of God's will for our lives. God has planned out everything and His plans for our lives are better than the world. The future is looking good and brighter. Hope is the goodness that keeps us in this love that God has abundantly for us. There is no greater love than this. We will never know any love in all our lives other than the one that God expressed and demonstrated to us through Jesus Christ, our blessed Savior. "Greater love has no one than this, than to lay down one's life for his friends" (Jn. 15:13).

Beloved, love forever. Be blessed in this virtue. Combat the evils in the world with love. Stay grounded in peace. Joy. Peace. Goodness. Faith. Mercy. Hope. Long-suffering. Kindness. Gentleness. These are the love that continues to shine upon us. As we arise, God's love awakens us, and His glory shines through daily. The world can only attest to this love in us by how we act and treat others because, by their fruits, we will know them (Mt.7:16). Think. Listen. Love. Laugh. Hold no prisoners. Be free. Love is the best policy to have, and it keeps us forever in God's goodness.

You see, love carries us daily whether we realize this or not, and it is the essence of our being. Love is the soul of humanity, and hatred brings chaos to the soul. Love is an excellent virtue that we must strive to have in abundance, and it is not the sensual kind of love that the world glorifies themselves in because of their lustful taste in lifestyles. Love is the spirit that brings good tidings to our souls. When we have love in our hearts, there is nothing that we cannot do. Love is a motivator and an action that keeps doing, and it never could stop doing.

Christ is love, and since we radiate this love of Christ in us, we must show the same kind of love towards others. Love is the soul of humanity when we live together as one and not seeing flaws in one another. Love is the virtue that brings out the best in us daily when we channel our energy to live as God intended us to live together as one. Understand that there is no color, nationality, gender, or race with love because love does not look at all these things. Love is a perfect virtue that has zero flaws. We must operate daily, loving one another as God has loved us, showing kindness to everyone regardless of who they are. We must be patient with all we encounter and not judge anyone by their limitations, appearance, and status.

Humility is the essence of love, and love is the key to forgiveness "for love will cover a multitude of sins" (1Pt.4:8). Love does not judge others or boastful. Love brings us to a perfect union with God through humility, which is expressed in our daily lives in how we interact and engage with others. We are the representatives of

God on earth, and we must show the characters of God through our conduct expressly by genuine love.

Love is the best, and we need it daily to live this life filled with purpose and fulfill our God's given ministry. Love sustains us through the faith of God. It is a long-suffering virtue and flawless. Love is the only medicine that can cure all sicknesses and diseases. Love is the most powerful virtue besides being the greatest. Love is patient and kind because we are made in the image and the likeness of God. "Love has been perfected among us in this: that we may have boldness in the day of judgment; because as He is, so are we in this world" (1Jn.4:17).

We must learn to be patient with all. We must learn to extend this patience that comes from knowing God and His unconditional affections towards humankind. Love is kind because God is a gracious and compassionate God towards us. If we say that we belong to God, we must demonstrate this virtue in abundance. Through this love, we are known as the true children of God. Through this love, we draw the world to Christ and not by any other means. Through this love, the world is healed. Through this love, we live in unity with one another and take care of one another. Through this love, we continue victoriously. Through this love, we stand and have full assurance through faith in the Son.

Love is the perfection of all that Christ has made us be through this faith that brought salvation to us. Love is not a virtue that seeks to destroy others but builds up. When we love, we do all that is there to do. We understand. We lift others up. We encourage others and help when we are in the position to do so. You see, love can only shine the light of God in our lives when we truly follow in the footsteps of Christ. Love can only shine the light of God in our lives when we embody all that is good and walk in God's commandments, and the first goes like this, "You shall love the Lord your God with all your heart, with all your soul, with all your strength, and with all your mind,' and 'your neighbor as yourself" (Lk.10:27).

Love keeps us when everything else fails in this mercy, in this goodness, and this light of God daily. Love can never be boastful because true love is founded in Christ, and it is the love that perfects and keep us humble and not to think highly of ourselves. "For I say, through the grace given to me, to everyone who is among you, not to think of himself more highly than he ought to think, but to think soberly, as God has dealt with each one a measure of faith" (Rm.12:3).

Moreover, grace stepped in, and faith embraced us through this unfailing love of Christ. So, think about it whenever we are in the assembly of those who are unlovable to us. Let us show this divine love to everyone, which opens the channel of greatness. May God continue to give us the understanding that provides us with true knowledge in the mighty name of Jesus. Amen.

VERSE FIVE

---✤---

LOVE IS SELFLESS

Love does not behave rudely, does not seek its own, is not provoked, thinks no evil.

The important thing about love is that it is a perfect virtue. It is a perfect virtue that seeks the good of all regardless of who they are. God's love is not restricted to an individual, community, people, or nation, and that is how our mindset should be programmed. Love is the most excellent virtue, and that is who Christ is to us every day. Have we ever wondered if God could count all our evil ways against us how we will be able to stand?

God's love is perfect and unconditional. True love should be unconditional and flawless. If we love one another as God loved us unconditionally, we will live free of burdens. We would live peacefully and conscience-free. We would live without watching our backs. Love is the cement that can only fix the cracks in the foundation. The foundation will continue to be shaken because of a lack of love for one another and fear of God. Love does no evil.

It does not seek to get even against one another. It is a virtue that shows God's heart, compassion, mercy, and graciousness towards us by Christ Jesus. We must love a little every day and watch the shifting in the atmosphere and the environment go better and higher for good. The world is clouded and clothed in wickedness, and until that is taken off and replaced with love, wickedness and other evil things will continue to be the norms.

Love conquers all. Love sustains us all in this journey through the Son. Love heals us all and makes us one in Christ. There is no room for rudeness, resentfulness, judgment, discrimination, racism, tribalism, and as the list goes on, when there is the existence of perfect love, which cast out all fears.

Beloved, love is not selfish but selfless. Love is not arrogant, but it is the spirit of humility. Love is always seeking good and helping others. Love is the grace that carries us along day by day in this journey. Love is the comfort that God has given to us to keep us steady and grounded in this journey through faith and grace. Love is always caring for others. Love is kind towards others. Love is continuously extending helping hands to others. "And the King will answer and say to them, 'Assuredly, I say to you, inasmuch as you did it to one of the least of these My brethren, you did it to Me" (Mt .25:40) is the essence of great love. This verse is the basis for love and kindness found in Jesus Christ.

We cannot say anything otherwise but live our lives in Christ and what Christ's words indicated. We must show others this love that radiates from the Father to the Son and from the Son to us through Holy Spirit's help. Love is the light of God in us that lets us knows that we truly belong to God. Love is the inner soul that touches humanity all over, and the ability demonstrates it for us to express this light from God directly to others not only through our words but by our actions. Love does not judge anyone. It is not rude because it is a perfect virtue. "Love will cover a multitude of sins" (1Pt.4:8). It heals and brings unity and harmony to all. It is the true virtue that brings the light of God into our lives and shines it so brightly that there is no denying that we are the children of God.

Beloved, we are indeed the light of the world (Mt.5:14) when we allow others to see God's light in us by the way we treat and speak to others, by the way, we honor God's laws, and by the way, we conduct ourselves in this world. Love is the greatest, and there can never be any virtue like it that is second to none because God's affairs are done through love by faith in Jesus Christ. God said, "I have loved you with an everlasting love; Therefore, with lovingkindness, I have drawn you" (Je.31:3). Otherwise, brethren, where do we think we would be without this eternal love of God through Christ to us?

Let us think about it. Let us think about God's unconditional love for us. Let us think about how God does not treat us as our sins deserve or repay us according to our iniquities (Ps.103:10). Let us think about how God continues to have mercy upon all our lives daily through His renewed mercy. Let us think about His kindness towards us. Let us think about this hope that we have in the Son and helps us to keep going and looking ahead to the future daily. Love is the essence of God because God is love(1Jn.4:16) and love is a powerful virtue that God has given to us to heal, combat hate, bring peace and harmony, and fellowship with one another in the unity of the Holy Spirit.

Thank God for the love that makes life worth living through the Son. Thank God for this fullness of God's head in our lives daily. God's mercy and goodness are the true love that God made around us daily to continue without frustration in this journey when we look up to Him, who is so kind and merciful towards us day by day. Beloved, increase in this virtue. Abound daily in it. Love is perfection through this grace that brings the glory of God to our lives in our weaknesses.

Love is a perfect virtue, and we must not keep being afraid. We are told in the Scripture that love casts out all fears, and the reason we still fear is that we have not been perfected by love(1Jn.4:18). When we love, we do not fear. When we love, we do not see the wrong that others do. We forgive expressly without holding grudges. Love operates on a different spiritual plane, which is why many cannot attain this gift because they are not of God.

Love is collective, and it occurs in a two-way street, and it is not into me and the ego. The tenet of love is humility, and humility is the virtue that also channels the blessings through faith. We can see how these virtues are interconnected with each other. Love is not self-seeking or possessive because it is full of understanding, trust, kindness, tolerance, and patience.

Beloved, God is love, and God's characters are expressed daily through His love for humankind. Love abides, and it is the greatest of all virtues because it keeps sustaining us even when we fall short of meeting the standards that God has for us every day. God does not judge us or condemn us the way we do to others. God is always forgiving, caring, and loving towards us. God is always faithful to us even when we turn away from Him and become unreasonable. God is slow to anger but abounding in mercy towards us; otherwise, how can we stand daily.

Love is the fountain of life and all that is good. Love is the virtue that shines the true knowledge of God to us by faith. Let us understand this virtue. Let us spend the time reflecting on the love of God towards us because there is no greater love than this; not even the love of a mother to her children or a husband to his wife or vice versa can take the place of this extraordinary, marvelous love that God has for us.

Love is a perfect virtue, and it manifests the essence of who God is, and we ought to follow in the same manner. Love is an excellent virtue, and it is the virtue that keeps working in us through faith for perfection. Love is the greatest, and we all need it to move along in our journeys and sustain us in our earthly stay. Love is a two-way street and does not seek revenge on others. It does not do teeth for tat. If we can only walk with God and allow Him to direct our paths in all that we do. Suppose we can allow God to change us from the inside and out. If we can allow God to perfect us, we will shine like the stars in the sky. Beloved, love is still missing in all our lives, and until we are filled with this abundance virtue, there will be no end to all the sorrows in the world. Where love is lacking, you can be sure that darkness and wickedness are the works we will see all around.

VERSE SIX

———————✤———————

LOVE IS THE TOKEN GESTURE

Love Does not rejoice in iniquity but rejoices in the truth.

Love is the vehicle that carries us daily in this world filled with sorrows, pain, and wickedness. Love is the life that gives us true meaning and purpose for our being. Love is the music that soothes the spirit and keeps us healed in our souls. Love is an excellent virtue that is always seeking the good of everyone regardless of who they are, and we must be filled with this virtue abundantly. Love is the truth that makes us free and the way we treat our fellow men.

Love is the expression of kindness and caring that we show towards others. It is how we walk in the footsteps of the Almighty God. Beloved, God is love, and we should emulate God's characteristics in all that we do for Him. We cannot be the children of God and do things that are contrary to His word. We cannot say that we are the children of God and walk with the devil and do the works of the devil. We cannot knowingly participate in discriminating and hating the children of God because of who they are.

Love is boundless. Love is the life that we have and the life that brings this glory of the Son to our lives. Love is the virtue that seeks the wellbeing of all and declares the unconditional and eternal love of the Father to us in the Son. Love every day without hesitation. Embrace without denouncing. Compassion without judgment. Justice without discrimination. God bless us as we continue to display the Christ in us through this great virtue. When we love, we are not intimidated. When we love, we speak the truth regardless of what it may cost us.

Love is a mutual understanding of the goodness between two people. Love is the token gesture that we express to others sincerely by actions and not by words only. When we express love by words only, love becomes a temporary thing that is superficial and not solid. Love can only endure when it is founded upon the understanding that when I give a little, and you give a little, and we all give a little, the universe will be a better place. Love rejoices in truth, and the truth is the virtue that also brings light that radiates from God. Love is the virtue that gives us the liberty that brings inner peace in Christ. Love does not rejoice in iniquity because it is the virtue that completes us perfectly through the grace of God.

Many lack this needed virtue to move mightily in the gifts of the Holy Spirit and their ministries, but they cannot move because they lack the love inside for others and the humility to carry them across to the finish line. "Where there is no vision, the people perish" (Pr.29:18 KJV). Love opens our spiritual eyes of understanding in this journey through faith. Love compels God to move for us when we need it most through faith, grace, and the mercy of Jesus Christ. Love is essential, and without it, we fall short of all that God has ordained us to be in this life. Love is the ministry at heart that moves us to be Christ-like every day. God is love (1Jn .4:16), and this cannot be stress enough. "But if anyone loves God, this one is known by Him"(1Cor.8:3).

What a vital virtue love truly is. Love is good for the growth of our spirituality in this journey. The more love we have in abundance, the more we grow faster at an alarming rate spiritually beloved. Love is the heart of Christ for His church on earth. Live and learn. Love and laugh. Joy and peace. Do not forget to abound in this special gift that God has given to us expressly through the Son, and it is the sunshine in our hearts daily. Thank God for this virtue daily. We all need a little bit of love to make this world a better place for everyone, regardless of who they are.

Truth is the essence of love, and love seeks to do just that. Love is the virtue that makes us whole because it is a lighthouse. Love is always seeking and prevailing in righteousness and in all that is good. Love cannot be evil because God is love and the light that surrounds us all around. God is the love that shines true in our lives, and we walk in this perfect love, truth, and justice every day.

When we love, we have no room for the unrighteous works of the devil. Love brings unity and unity, harmony when we walk in light and truth daily.

Love does not, and it will never rejoice in evil or unrighteous works of the devil displayed by others. Love is the true virtue that holds us dear and near God when we bear the fruits that speak true to whom God has made us be. Love can never be what we want it to be in our wicked ways because it is a spirit of kindness, of compassion, of mercy, of grace, of the truth, of goodness and the list are endless. Let us be filled with love daily showing others that we are genuine disciples and the children of Christ. Love shines the light that no man can turn off because of the God who lives in us daily.

Unconditional love is the love that is built solid, and nothing else could shake that. Let us have the love that builds up. Let us have the love that seeks the good of others. Let us have the love that rejoices in the truth. Let us have the love that makes hopes the joy of our future. Let us build up one another day by day and stop the disunity that causes hatred among us. Love carries us through our earthly stay, and we must know there is no substitute for love.

Love is the virtue that wins out every day, no matter the challenges. Love is a uniter and not a divider. Love is peace and not war. Love is the harmony that brings this heavenly peace that radiates and saturates our lives. Let us desire more love and give it to others the way Christ has taught us. Love is the fruit and the virtue that speaks true to our identity in Christ because we cannot say that we belong to Christ and then do the works of the devil. Be rest assured that this virtue is non-negotiable because it is a commandment from God.

We must love God primarily and our neighbor as ourselves. Love seeks good always, and no matter the trials, it abides with faith and hope forever and ever. Beloved, understand that love does not change and will continue to exist after everything is said and done because God's love for us is consistent. It is long-suffering and endures. It is what sustains our journey, and it is the truth that we live for the life that brings God to us while we are still clothed in this earthly body.

Love is the essence of the life we have been given, and God's love is genuine and not on the surface as men. Truth wins, and justice prevails, and love is the route by which these are done. Love should not be partial. Furthermore, we must treat one another equally. Agape love for God's children should reign in all our lives day by day.

VERSE SEVEN

----------·❖·----------

LOVE IS AN EXCELLENT VIRTUE

Love bears all things, believes all things, hopes all things, endures all things.

And above all things have fervent love for one another, for love will cover a multitude of sins" (1Pt.4:8). Love is the virtue that brings perfection when we put on God's image and likeness and when we walk in His footsteps. Love is the fruit and the virtue that keeps shinning in our souls and letting the world know that we are indeed set apart and are the children of God. We cannot be the children of God with hate in our hearts, and that has already been established.

Love is a powerful virtue when we do as God has commanded us to do and not to walk like the world even though we are in the world, but we are not of the world (Jn.17:16). Love is all. There is nothing that it cannot conquer or overcome when we are filled with it. Love is the music that expresses the love of Christ in us, and in turn, we express and play this music back to others. When we walk in love, we walk in the abundance of God's Spirit because God is love, and that is one of His most excellent essences.

Love endures, and it bears. It hopes, and it believes. It is genuine, and it is solid and not built on the surface. It is the brainchild of everything that we do in this world. When we walk in the abundance of love, we begin to flourish and see the mighty hands of God in all that we do. Rest assured that the greatest of these is love, and where there is love, you can count on the overflow of blessings. God is love, and all that God does for us is because of His infinite love, mercy, and compassion towards us every day despite when we fall shorts of His glory, of His standards and expectations.

God's love is eternal because it bears and is patience. It seeks to correct and mold us. It aims to repair and transform us. Love is the key to the true transformation of the self because when we understand the love of Christ for us, we begin to appreciate the true meaning of the love that God has demonstrated to us through His only begotten Son, Jesus Christ. Beloved, let us follow God. Let us practice this perfect love that heals, brings peace, and gives true meaning to life in Jesus's name.

Love does not owe grudges. Love does not seek to get even. Love does not hate. Love does not bear false witness against anyone. Love does not see the skin color of others. Love does not judge anyone. Love is a long-suffering virtue that brings the goodness and the healings of God to our souls, and when we grasp that, we are ready to fulfill our God-ordained purpose from heaven. This virtue is a humongous virtue that continues to shine the glory of this God Jesus Christ upon all our lives. The fruits of love are found in goodness and patience. They are found in gentleness and kindness. They are found in joy, and the list keeps getting longer beloved.

Love is an excellent virtue that makes the grace of God rest upon all our lives through this faith in the Son. Love bears all things because "love covers the multitude of sins" (1Pt.4:8). It is the virtue of forgiveness and hope. It is the virtue that brings an abundance of grace to rest upon our lives through Christ Jesus. This truth frees us, and truth happens because of the love that God has demonstrated to us in His Son.

Beloved, love completes us in this journey; otherwise, how else can we stand before God daily? Thank God for this love that can bear our weaknesses through the grace of the Son. Thank God for this love that believes all things through the faith that was manifested to us in the Son of God because "God so loved the world that He gave His only begotten Son, that whoever believes in Him should not perish but have everlasting life" (Jn.3:16).

That is the eternal love that God has blessed us with, and we need not worry about anything. Love brings hope, and this hope is in Christ because the Christ in us daily is the hope of glory (Col.1:27). Hope gives us something to hold onto, and that something is the faith that we have in the Son. Hope is the future looking brighter for us daily in the Son because we are not without hope. In Christ, our hopes are built every day because of these beaming lights that shine daily in our lives through the Son. Love is the virtue that keeps us solid and brings God to us expressly through faith. We must be filled with love to know that God knows us.

We cannot claim to love God while our daily lives represent the opposite of love. Beloved, God will judge those who live life without this love severely one day and make no mistake about it. Practice love. Love without hesitation. Love is perfect when we stop being afraid and see the good in all of God's creations. You see, love is the power within us, and this power can do everything with faith in Christ. We must believe with all our hearts and trusts God with everything, no matter the trials that face us. Love stays forever true when we understand that God's love is constant and poured every day to lead and guide us in every step that we take in this journey. Love is the virtue that lasts forever when everything else fails, and we can always count on this unconditional love of God that never fails daily in our lives as mercy is renewed daily.

Love is the essence of life that we have, and that life is true in the Son of God. Love carries us steadily and faithfully no matter our circumstances.

Love is the virtue that bears all things, endures all things, protects, and it is our being, it is what guides our steps, it is what leads us in this journey, it is what embraces us, it is what gives us the hope for a better future with God in it, and it persevered us no matter the challenges. Love is the heart of ministry, and everyone must fulfill their purpose. Love is the key to building the nations and stop all the hurts that go on today. Imagine what this greatest virtue can do if we all could love a little bit more.

What a wonderful world we would have. What a unity on earth if we have love. God is the love that radiates in our lives every day and everything that we do. We must understand that love is an important virtue that upholds us in truth, character, and all we strive to do for others through humility. Love is not through words but what we do to others by action only. It is expressed by the way we respond or do not respond to others. It is the way we extend help genuinely to others without expecting anything in return. It is the kind soul that dwells in our spirit and has the abundance of God's characters. It is the unspoken words that heal the wounded souls. It is the way we talk and interact with others.

Beloved, understand that love can only be expressed when we take the initiative to walk with God blamelessly and "inasmuch as you did it to one of the least of these My brethren, you did it to Me "(Mt.25:40) is the highest form of love. Walk in love. Express it through action. Show kindness to others. Mercy is the partner of love, and let us show that all the time. Compassion is the music that brings joy. Extend it. Embrace kindness. Talk peacefully. Walk in God's glory, and we will not lack in any good things that God has destined for us.

VERSE EIGHT

LOVE NEVER FAILS

Love never fails. But whether there are prophecies, they will fail; whether there are tongues, they will cease; whether there is knowledge, it will vanish away.

Love is an enduring virtue, and it cannot fail. Love is the hope for the future, and we must hold onto it. You see, when everything else fails and stops, love is sure. It sustains us from one realm of glory to another and from one spiritual level to another higher spiritual level. It does not matter how spiritually gifted we are; these gifts will eventually end, but love is eternal.

It transcends everything that we could ever imagine from generation to generation. Love is a powerful virtue that we all need daily to stand before God through faith in Christ Jesus. Love makes us through faith by grace in the Son, and it is an important virtue that keeps shinning God's countenance of peace upon us no matter the trials that we go through every day. Love is so important, and we must strive to walk in love, live by it, and embrace it to live a divine purposeful life filled with the knowledge of God, Jesus Christ.

Love endures. It cannot fail because God cannot fail, and that is a proven fact. The love of God towards us is sure and is consistent daily. It is what we live for. It is what helps us to keep pressing forward. It is our lifeline. It is the light that shines in the darkness. Beloved, the spiritual gifts we are endowed with we surely be brought to an end one day when God decides enough is enough, but God's unfailing love is sure every day. God's unfailing love is what keeps our feet on the ground and the reason we live and carry-on day by day. Embrace love. Give it. Do not hesitate to express it. Be kind.

Love is our heartbeats. It is what gives meaning to living and our essence of being. When everything else fails, love will never because it is the life we have in our Savior, Jesus Christ. Love is what draws us nearer to God through faith by the mercy of the Son of God. Love is the light in our lives that drives away the darkness. Love is the channel by which we hold firmly through faith in the Lord. Beloved, this virtue is a powerful virtue that opens the pathway to goodness and prosperity in all our lives when we hold onto love through this faith found in the Son.

There is no substitute for love. Nothing can replace this virtue. It is a must-have and must keep virtue. Love is the virtue that can only build us up spiritually in Christ through our faith in the Son. We must strive to have this excellent virtue rest upon us through the grace of this one God: The Father, the Son, and the Holy Spirit. Love never fails because when everything else does, it remains. It remains to make us stand bodily daily and in confidence. Love is the greatest of all the virtues. It does not fail or change. It does not fade or lose its value. Love is founded upon the mercy that God has demonstrated to us through Jesus Christ.

Love is an action. It must be demonstrated by actions, not only through words. Love is what carries us daily in this journey, and through love, we have the abundance of God's Spirit. Everything God does for us is motivated by the love of the Son, and we must understand that and appreciate that greatly. Love is the light that keeps shinning in us for the world to see Jesus in us. We cannot kill this love just like anyone will not stop this light of God from shining in our lives. We must abide in the Son. Love is the virtue that heals both spiritually and otherwise. Love is the virtue that brings hope in dare situations.

Love is the forgiveness that we extend to the wrongs that others do to us. Love is the healings that God has given to us to withstand anything in the world. We must have this virtue beloved to know that we truly belong to God. God is love, and love is God. We cannot separate this virtue from God; otherwise, we will not be alive today. Love stands firmly when everything fails. Love never fails.

Love is a constant virtue, and we must understand that it stays after everything else fails. That is why there is no substitute for it. It is a healing medicine as well as perfecter through the grace of God. It is a super virtue that shows the mind of Christ, and since we have the mind of Christ, we are endowed with this gracious beloved gift from the Father through the Son to us. Love is like no other virtue. It does not fear. It does not judge. It does not condemn. It does not speak evil of anyone. It does not hold grudges or keep records of wrongs. It is the spiritual essence of light that permeates towards us from God.

Understand that when everything else fails, love remains because that is the mercy of God that keeps us afloat daily on this earth; otherwise, we are finished. Love is the essence of our life, and through it, we came to be because of God's love for us. We must strive to love with all our hearts, and when we understand the first commandment, we are nearer to God than we think every day. Love defines who we are, and it is the fruit that shows the Christ in us and not through any other means, but many refuse to believe that because their hearts are evil.

You see, the haters have the same fate as unbelievers and murderers. Let us not make any mistake about that. Love does not fear because perfection can only flourish in us when we walk in the purity of heart and have the qualities of God in us. Love is good, and it brings more of the Spirit into our lives and causes us to have this tremendous and affectionate relationship with God through His Spirit. Let us try love. Let us start with a little here and a little there today. Let us heal the world with love. Let us come together as one and as God has intended for us to live as one. God will judge everyone, and our responsibility is to love one another and not judge. May we continue to flourish in this virtue and be filled with more of Christ through the power of His Spirit.

VERSE NINE

―――――⟡―――――

LOVE CONQUERS ALL

For we know in part and we prophesy in part.

Knowledge is ongoing, and we must never stop trying and striving for the knowledge that brings understanding. We must open our hearts to receive from God and learn from Him. Understanding is the gift that opens the door to great spiritual enlightenment. We are still learning and perfecting ourselves every day. We do not have the whole puzzle pieces together, but there will surely come a time when everything will be made clear to us.

In the meantime, let us seek the face of God continuously. Let us look for God and faithfully seek Him to be rewarded because God is a rewarder of those who diligently seek Him. Beloved, we know in part, and we prophesy in part because we have yet to understand who God is completely. We are yet to understand how God does things and having a little bit here and a little bit there is not the whole picture, and that is why we must never stop seeking God. Deep calls unto the deep (Ps.42:7). Let us thirst for more of God and open our hearts to God to come in. Love is the channel through faith that we can be enlightening in the knowledge of God.

Nothing lasts forever except love. Love is the gift of life that stays with us from generation to generation. When everything else perishes, love endures. Love conquers. Love remains. Love builds. Love heals. Love is the virtue of hope that makes the future brighter. We must understand that. The gifts of God are summoned up in this virtue. We must learn love to live in our God's ordained destiny. Love is the driving force behind the universe, and it is built on the notion of this life that transcends all things. Love is embedded in our DNA, and it is the absolute gift that gives birth to our nature.

Love is the virtue that not only enlightens but gives us the courage to build upon ourselves in a way that speaks true to the nature of our being. Love carries us when we live in this peace, in this joy, in this simplicity, and in this humility that comes from knowing the one and only God, Jesus Christ. Beloved, we cannot claim to know it all because the life they say is not a bed of roses, but love is the roses that bring beautiful aroma to our lives. Love is the grace that makes life worth living. Love is good, and it originated from God through Christ to us. Love is not as the world defines it to be. It is more than that. It is more than sensual and lust. Love is the spiritual aspect of our being that connects us to our Maker daily, and that is why God is love.

We cannot separate who God is from this virtue. God wants us to love our neighbors as ourselves. God wants us to be kind to others. God wants us to treat others as we would ourselves. God wants us to bear with one another. God wants us to take care of one another and be our brother's keepers. God wants us to be loving towards one another. God wants us to be sympathetic towards one another. God wants us to put the needs of others above ourselves. Beloved, "And the King will answer and say to them, 'Assuredly, I say to you, inasmuch as you did it to one of the least of these My brethren, you did it to Me" (Mt.25:40) is the basis upon which true love is founded.

Love is flawless. We must know that we are imperfect people, and because of this eternal love of God, we are drawn to God's throne of mercy daily. What we have in part is not guaranteed, but love lasts forever. "For I am persuaded that neither death nor life, nor angels nor principalities nor powers, nor things present nor things to come, nor height nor depth, nor any other created thing, shall be able to separate us from the love of God which is in Christ Jesus our Lord" (Rm.8:38–39). God is the love in our hearts and the love that drives our passions daily to do what we need to do in this ministry of love, mercy, grace, encouragement, hope, peace, and joy.

Love is all, and through it, we have this beautiful faith that shines in our lives through Jesus Christ, our blessed

Savior. We know in part and prophecy in part because nothing is complete without love. Love is the driving force behind everything that we do. Love is at the top of everything and cannot be separated from life. We have not even begun to know who God is. We think we already have everything figured out, and then we discover there are many things we still do not know, and that is why we must keep asking, seeking, and knocking (Mt.7:7). Beloved, "for who has known the mind of the Lord that he may instruct Him?" But we have the mind of Christ" (1Cor.2:16).

We must understand that we are imperfect vessels that God uses daily, and we are prone to errors, but God is faithful. Beloved, God can never lie. "God is not a man, that He should lie, nor a son of man, that He should repent. Has He said, and will He not do? Or has He spoken, and will He not make it good?" (Nm.23:19). "Let God be true but every man a liar" (Rm.3:4).

Let us keep working out our salvation and keep pressing forward because perfection is not and cannot be attained by our efforts, and it is only the grace of God that keeps us afloat in this journey through the unconditional love of the Son. Love happens to us, and God continues to bless and use us to His glory, and yet we have still not reached the level of perfection because we get it wrong most times, but that is why the grace of God perfects our weaknesses.

Love is the umbrella by which we stand daily, and God uses us as He sees fits. So, we must learn to humble ourselves and not be filled with the ego. We must learn to be obedient and yield to God because we still have a long road to travel to reach our destination, but love is incredible. Love is the strength that infused the grace of God in us and held us on God's shoulder. We are still on a journey and walking with God, day by day and should take nothing for granted, but we must keep seeking the face of God. Beloved, even what we think we know is not guaranteed, and we must wait and hold onto the end to see the whole picture at large. We must do all that pleases God and strive for excellence. Love is sure when we have faith in the Son and hold onto it.

VERSE TEN

---·❦·---

LOVE BRINGS PERFECTION

But when that which is perfect has come, then that which is in part will be done away.

We do not know anything and everything, and our understanding is still like trying to put the pieces of the puzzles back together. Let us be on God's side and learn from Him. Complete understanding comes when we are willing to undertake this journey with God and rejoice in it. We must understand that we do not have everything tucked in, and we must continue to strive for the best through the grace of God.

Knowledge is the key to understanding, and until we open our hearts to receive instructions from God, we are limited in our understanding. May God give us great insight into this spiritual understanding that shines knowledge and gives us wisdom. We prophesy in part because we do not have all the answers. We are susceptible to errors as humankind, and a little bit here and a little bit there does not give us a complete picture.

There will come a time when everything will be made clear and with perfect clarity but for now, let us abide in Christ until that day comes. Let us love and flourish in this virtue. Love carries us through faith to the throne of the Master, and what is perfect can only come when we live room for understanding and gain the knowledge of God from our initiative and encounter with Him. Love is the virtue that brings perfection through the grace of this incredible and amazing Jesus. Do not forget that as long as you live in this world.

We fear because we have not been made perfect in love. "There is no fear in love, but perfect love casts out fear because fear involves torment. But he who fears has not been made perfect in love" (1Jn.4:18). When we love, fear is cast out. Fear is what keeps us in the dark. Love is the virtue that combats that which is in part will be done away, which is fear. Love brings perfection when we abide in Christ and His Spirit. Let us yield ourselves to God daily in obedience and righteousness. Love perfects us truly when we walk with God daily. God can only be worshipped in Spirit and truth (Jn.4:24), and the essence of who this God is to humankind is founded on no other person but in the Son.

That which is perfect has come, and we have embraced it through faith. That which is perfect is the Son who is without no sin. That which is perfect is the love that radiates from the Son directly from the Father. Love has cast out the fears that held us in bondage. Darkness must give way for light to shine. The glory of the Son has genuinely risen upon us as we embrace God through the Son by faith daily. Love is the channel by which this is attained. Love is a great virtue that every child of God must be filled with. Love is the humility that keeps us serving others with excellent service because of the love of Christ that compels us daily. Love is the token and the gratitude in our hearts daily for all that God continues to do for us in the Son. That which is perfect can continue to enlighten us and the grace to carry us in this journey that we embark on through the help of the Spirit.

Rest assured that God's love is what is keeping us daily in the mercy of the Son. How else can what is perfect hold firm in our lives? Beloved, give glory to God every day for this perfection in love. Give glory to God for this banner of God's love surrounding all our lives. Perfection is through the grace of God that is embedded in love. Look no further. Jesus has done it for us. Rejoice. Proclaim. Shout. Skip. God is love, and through this love, we live and make this love known to others through our examples and holy conduct in the world. "By this, all will know that you are My disciples if you have love for one another" (Jn.13:35).

Many think that they know all that is to know, but they are mistaken. Let us be assured that we do not have it hundred percent in this journey, and understanding is something that we must keep striving for to reach the knowledge and receive the fullness of God, the Father, the Son, and the Holy Spirit. We are still drinking from a half-filled cup and should take nothing for granted because perfection comes when we are willing to learn from God.

Completeness comes when we are eager to do what God tells us to do and walk in His commandments and until that which is part disappears, we are still bound in our spiritual understanding and limitation. We must do all that is to follow God and receive this wisdom that only God can give to us, and wisdom brings knowledge and understanding to us. Let us open our hearts to God daily. Love is the virtue that does that through faith in the Son. Strive for excellence. Strive for the knowledge that improves our understanding of Christ. Strive to be the best individual that showcases the love and the light of God in the world, and only then can we know. Perfection comes with understanding. Beloved, quest for perfection. Thirst for it. Desire it. Understanding is the gift of hope, and perfection is the virtue that brings the life of purpose and total completeness. We must strive for genuine understanding so that these partial things can become irrelevant.

VERSE ELEVEN

LOVE DRIVES OUR LIVES

When I was a child, I spoke as a child, I understood as a child, I thought as a child; but when I became a man, I put away childish things.

Beloved, there is a time for everything under heaven (Ec.3:1–8). We go through various stages in life and growth, but we must understand when enough of something is enough, and it is time for improvement or moves along from one point to another point or from one level to another level. Some people have not figured that out yet. Some people are still in the same spot and refuse to move even when they know it is time to push forward. We cannot undermine the strength that God has given to us. We cannot put ourselves down if we want to make headway in this journey. Beloved, there is time for everything. We do not jump because others want us to. We do things based on the appropriate time, and God leading us to do them. With that being said and putting this out there. Let us continue to talk about this incredible and humongous virtue.

Spiritual maturity is the key to knowledge and understanding. Spiritual understanding brings the knowledge of God. Spiritual things can only be revealed and received in the Spirit and not in the flesh, and once we understand that, we are ready to forge ahead in this journey. "But God has revealed them to us through His Spirit. For the Spirit searches all things, yes, the deep things of God" (1Cor.2:10). Let us strive for spiritual maturity, and it is time to shed the childishness that holds many backs and limits them from reaching their destination and fulfilling their purpose.

There comes a time in a man's life when he has to know when enough is enough and when to take things seriously. We must forge ahead with determination and maturity. We must understand that there is time and place for everything. We must know that there is a difference between spiritual levels. We must strive to reach our God's given best in all our undertakings for God. We must stop being complacent and strive to go where no one else dares to go.

"Then He said to His disciples, "The harvest truly is plentiful, but the laborers are few" (Mt.9:37). Let us ride on and be zealous for God every day. "Deep calls unto deep at the noise of Your waterfalls; All Your waves and billows have gone over me" (Ps.42:7). Let the deep calls unto the deep in our lives now. Spiritual maturity is the vehicle to enlighten ourselves about our spiritual surroundings and drawing nearer to God in Spirit and truth.

Spiritual maturity happens when we are serious and passionate about God, Jesus Christ, and we cannot grow when we fall apart and refuse to take on and tackle the challenges and the issues we encounter daily. Love is perfect when we strive to live in this God's given life and fulfill our destiny according to God's plans for our lives. We must understand when to stop the childish behavior that takes us ten steps backward spiritually.

Love is all. It is the engine that drives everything that we do in this journey. Love is the life that is so precious, and we must never for one second take it for granted. We must appreciate this love that God had demonstrated to us when He gave us His Only begotten Son, Jesus Christ. Jesus Christ is the love of God's life. He is the One that God sacrificed for the forgiveness of our sins. There is no greater love (Jn.15:13) demonstrated to all humankind other than the one that God the Father has shown through Jesus Christ (Rm.5:8).

Love drives our lives. It is the affection that God has put into all His creations on earth, and it is now left for us to continue in that love which God has given to us by living up to God's expectation in this aspect. Love is the universe that we live in because God made this universe out of love spoken through His word and by His word only. There is time to act like children, but the time has now come for us all to grow up and see this bigger picture of God's love for us, and it continues to spread from one generation to another through Christ Jesus.

Love is the greatest, and we must continue to show it through our actions and not only through words. Love is the essence of life that continues in the world after everything else vanishes. Without it, we are nothing. Without it, we are not fit to be called God's creatures. Without it, we are dead spiritually. Without it, we cannot see clearly. Without it, we are just wandering about without directions. Love daily and combat the evils in the world with this healing virtue that God has given to humanity.

Some people do not understand when enough is enough and that there will come a time that we must grow up and face reality. Everything has its own time and season, and love is a perfecter. Let us strive to be the best that God has made us be. Let us live this meaningful life filled with love that expresses the Christ in us to others. You see, grown men take responsibility for their actions, which is not the case with a child. So, in this, we forged ahead to greater glory and a greater understanding that love happens to us all through the person of Jesus Christ.

Spiritual stuff is for the matured in Christ and not for babes(1Cor.3:2–3). Understanding of God comes with total and daily devotion. We have not yet reached that stage, knowing that the learning of God is to continue seeking Him. A child and a man's understanding are different in significant ways. When we are children, we are still learning, and as we grow, we grow through the knowledge that God gives to us, and we are shaped through that understanding.

Beloved, our understanding is still in the working progress mode, and we have not yet arrived at perfection. Perfection comes when we take on Christ and understand His mind, and love is the channel through faith by which we can do that. Love is the gift of enlightenment and the power of God that is immersed in us, and nothing compares to it. Love is the greatest gift that we can have, yet many are still struggling to receive it.

"To everything, there is a season, A time for every purpose under heaven: A time to be born, And a time to die; A time to plant, And a time to pluck what is planted; A time to kill, And a time to heal; A time to break down, And a time to build up; A time to weep, And a time to laugh; A time to mourn, And a time to dance; A time to cast away stones, And a time to gather stones; A time to embrace, And a time to refrain from embracing; A time to gain, And a time to lose; A time to keep, And a time to throw away; A time to tear, And a time to sew; A time to keep silence, And a time to speak; A time to love, And a time to hate; A time of war, And a time of peace"(Ec.3:1–8).

Everything has its own time, as you see. We must know that we do not yet know anything that we think we know about God, and our understanding of who God is still limited. Let us keep striving for this perfection till we arrive. Love is the avenue that can make this happen.

VERSE TWELVE

———— ✤ ————

LOVE IS THE SOURCE OF LIFE

For now, we see in a mirror, dimly, but then face to face. Now I know in part, but then I shall know just as I also am known.

Our hindsight is still very much clouded, and everything is not picture perfect because we are still humans, and we have yet to reach perfection. However, rest assured that perfection comes through abiding in Christ, and love is the vehicle upon which that is built. Let us continue to walk in love and God's commandments. Let us continue to shine as the light that we are in the Son. We cannot be disciples of Christ and lack love in our hearts. Understanding is the virtue that brings the glory of God when we open our hearts to receive knowledge.

Love is the source of life. Hold onto that life every day and live this very moment with gratitude to God. Love is the virtue that moves us to be the person God has ordained us to be in this life. Destiny fulfillment is tied with this virtue, and many have not grasped that beloved. What we see in a mirror dimly is due to our lack of ingenuity, and with lack of ingenuity comes despair. We cannot see the total package of our being in a sense without this virtue. We think we got it all worked out and tucked in, but we do not know anything. We must get to the point of realization that with love comes the freedom from above, which gives birth to greatness in our journeys. Love is the key to fulfilling God's given purpose and destiny. May we continue to strive for excellence in Christ through love and faith in Jesus Christ. Love enlightens us and sheds God's grace on us.

What we see in a mirror is an illusion. Perfection comes through grace by this love God has demonstrated to us in the Son. Love makes perfect because we are imperfect people. Love is the virtue that cast out fears, which cast out doubts, which cast out racism, which cast out discord, which cast out all the things that bring imperfections. Love is a perfect virtue, and by it, we can hold onto this life that God has given to us. No one is righteous but Christ, but through this love, we obtain perfection through this grace in Christ through the Holy Spirit's help. Now I know in part, but I shall know just as I am known that love completes us absolutely through the mercy of God; otherwise, how can we stand in this world.

How can we live if it was not for the mercy of this God, Jesus Christ? To know in part is a half-cup full, but we are made whole through this love—we are known just as we are known through this love, just as we are made to stand. The Christ in us is the glory that shines daily through this love. Completeness is found in knowing and abiding in Christ and not by any other means. No one is one hundred percent on this journey. Love happens to us all through this grace that God has made manifest to us by faith in the person of Jesus Christ. We are the imperfect people that God must shine His glory upon through Christ Jesus.

Perfection is through this love that casts out all fears. Perfection is through this grace that brings this saving faith. Perfection is knowing who God is to us; otherwise, how can we stand in this journey. Love is the virtue that brings goodness to us and makes us perfect through this grace of God in Christ Jesus. We cannot be deceived. An illusion is a lie, but true love is found in the life that Christ has given to us. What we see in a mirror and the man looking back at us is a reflection that does not provide the total picture of our being, but with love comes perfection in Christ. With love, we are made perfect by this Christ. With love, we can live this God's given life.

We can move in this life, in this ministry, and this journey with love. God knows who we are, and our destiny is in His hands. God is the all-knowing God. He is the God who knows our beginning to the end. We must rest assured about that and live this very moment, right now, this present time, with the knowledge of that. Love embraces us in the bosom of our mighty God. Love is the most essential of all the virtues, and without it, we cannot stand firm in this life.

We have not yet gotten to the stage of complete knowledge and understanding, and what we think we know is not the final, but a taste at its best while we wait to eat the whole meal in the end. Let us understand that no one can claim to know everything because we are all working towards perfection, which cannot happen immediately. It takes to form a little bit at a time. We must continue to learn and listen because that is how we grow spiritually. We must continue to improve on ourselves every day and surrender to God.

Humility is the channel through which we must pass to attain this perfection. Understanding is the true light when we know God's expectations. Let us strive for excellence in all that we do for God. Let us continue to walk in this love, in truth, and with God, and only then can we begin to see ourselves the way God sees us, and we must continue to yield ourselves to God. Love is the mercy that we receive, and God's unconditional love is the only thing that is perfect and makes sense to us. Perfection comes with the grace of God, and transformation happens when we have the mindset of God and take on His characteristics. You see, we still have many roads to travel to arrive at our destinations. We still have many learnings to do because it does not end with one try.

VERSE THIRTEEN

—————— ❧ ——————

LOVE IS THE GREATEST

And now abide faith, hope, love, these three; but the greatest of these is love.

Faith, hope, and love are the essences of goodness. They keep us afloat in the Son daily. We cannot lose sight of these three friends or amigos, as you all would say. Beloved, faith and hope carry us steadily daily through this priceless grace that God has made manifest in all the believers' lives through this Jesus Christ, our Savior. Faith speaks love in all our lives, yet it is love that is more abundantly through God's love for all of humankind. "For God so loved the world that He gave His only begotten Son, that whoever believes in Him should not perish but have everlasting life" (Jn.3:16). That is an absolute and unconditional love that God expressed to us all through faith and by faith only in the Son. Faith works with love, and it stands parallel to it, yet it is the virtue of love that is the greatest.

We must hold onto these three virtues daily. We must not let go of God's abundance of grace that is shown and demonstrated to us all through the love of the Son. Love carries us through mercy, which is an undeniable fact in Christ. Love is the banner that solely puts us all in God's graces day by day; otherwise, where would we be? Love is the greatest, and there are no other virtues like it in this life or the life to come. Everything that God has ever done is motivated by this great love for His Son and the Son for us. Love is the life that we have every day and must be appreciated. Love is the grace that gives birth to this new life in the Spirit that draws us closer to God by this beautiful faith.

Faith, hope, and love, as well as the other virtues, are intertwined. They cannot be separated; however, we try to do that; you find that they are intertwined and constantly collaborating along with each other, but love is the source of all the virtues. Love gives power to the other virtues. Love is an empowering virtue that keeps us in this goodness and the mercy of God no matter how badly we keep behaving. Beloved, that is why God's love is eternal, and nothing separates us from this sweet and everlasting love that God has for all His children. Abide in faith, live in hope and love. Increase in all areas and have more in love.

God's ministry starts with love and humility, but faith and hope are not far behind. While faith gives us this life, this life cannot be attained without this divine love of God. Love is the channel by which we receive the faith that gives us life in Christ and by Christ only. Let us begin to understand this concept, beloved precious one in Christ. Love stands fully to fulfill us in this journey when faith is working, but it must work with faith. That is why love is an essential and very crucial virtue to have in abundance. Many perish because they do not know, and when we do not know, we lack the gravity to stand in spiritual understanding. Do you get My concept, beloved?

Faith, hope, and love are the virtues that bring us heaven when we faithfully follow Christ. Faith works with hope and love, and these are intertwined with each other. Faith is the life that never dies in Christ, and hope is the lighthouse of faith, and these two need each other to form a perfect union for our good, and love is the sum of it all. Love is the reason for faith and this eternal hope that we have. Beloved, love is the greatest virtue because it is the gift of life that God gave us in Christ through faith. "For God so loved the world that He gave His only begotten Son that whoever believes in Him should not perish but have everlasting life" (Jn.3:16).

That is the greatest love for us, and no one can ever show us the kind of love that God has demonstrated through the Son.

Love speaks true to who God is to us. His essence is love. He is the epitome of this love that rest and radiates in our lives every day. That is why we must reflect the essence of who Christ is by the way we treat one another, how we care for and about one another, by our attitude towards one another and others, and through our generosity. You see, love is the life that many has rejected because they are evil and their works are evil like their father, the devil.

Let faith abide. Let hope transport us on the wings of faith to reach our God's given potentials. Faith is the key to destiny fulfillment, and we cannot accomplish anything without faith. Faith is the virtue that leads us directly to the heartbeat of God through Christ. We must be full of faith if we want to have a lasting relationship with God, and hope is the lighthouse of faith. It keeps us grounded and assured in Christ. It gives us the strength to continue through the power of the Holy Spirit. It reminds us of what we know and have in Christ and never to let go even in the middle of the trials and the tribulations.

Many lack these virtues, which is why we see the desperation to attain an authentic life. How can a life be worth living when it lacks the prerequisite of what we must have to be fully and spiritually connected to God through Christ? Love carries us repeatedly despite our imperfections. It shines the mercy of God through and through no matter how badly we behave, and that is why nothing can ever separate us from the love of Christ (Rm.8:35). Faith, hope, and love will abide forever, and love will remain after everything is said and done through faith, and we must never give up on hope, beloved.

We cannot miss heaven with these three virtues. They are always seen and working together for our perfection. So, hang on to them as we do with dear life. Faith, hope, and love are the best virtues, and we cannot go wrong with these three. Love is the life that we have and the heart of the other virtues. Love is the virtue that keeps shinning the glory of God, the Father, and the Son to us through the power of the Holy Spirit. We must keep learning about this virtue until we fully understand it because it is not lust or sensual. It is not about engaging ourselves inappropriately.

Love is the divine gift from God to us, and until we experience this kind of love, we cannot express it to others. Love is the light that lives in our souls, and in this light, we can draw others to the One who is the true light in our lives. That is why love is everything. Love conquers all and heals. Love fixes the brokenhearted. Love can do what we need because it is a virtue like faith that never stops working and doing for our good and perfection.

Love is the sum of it all, and when we realize that we need love to move in our spiritual gifts and offices, we will desire to have more of this excellent gift that God has bequeathed to us. Hope is the lighthouse of faith, and these are great partners also. They bring total restoration and a great future. "Eye has not seen, nor ear heard, nor have entered into the heart of man The things which God has prepared for those who love Him" (1Cor.2:9).

Beloved, faith is working for our well-being. Faith is a gift of resurrection and the eternal life that only God offers us through His only begotten Son, Jesus Christ. Faith is the channel by which we are made the children of God and accepted into His family. We need faith to stand and to please God. We need faith to live the victorious life that Christ has given us. Faith is the key to living this God-given and ordained life forever, and hope is never far behind these two. Hope is the lighthouse of faith. It is the brighter future ahead and the better plans that God has prepared for us.

We cannot let go of this hope; otherwise, for what else do we hope? For what else do we live? What is other life available out there? Hope is the gift of faith, and as long as we have this and hold on tight to it, we can move forward no matter the perils of life or the difficulties of everyday lives. God cannot and will never quit on us because His love for us is unconditional. God's love is the life that keeps us sustained throughout this challenging journey.

Let us show love to others regardless of who they are. When we judge others because of who they are, we judge the One who created us all. Furthermore, we must understand that we are not going to escape the same judgment and condemnation. Love is the soul of the body, and it gives life to everything that we do. Love reflects Jesus Christ in us, and through it, we are known. Love shows that we are the children and servants of God by the way we act and do unto others. Love is the virtue as well as the fruit that genuinely shines the light and the glory of God upon us.

We must endeavor to walk in this light of God daily. Beloved, do not hesitate for one second about loving others as yourselves. God's commandment is clear on this, and it is non-negotiable. "Owe no one anything except to love one another, for he who loves another has fulfilled the law" (Rm.13:8). May God bless us all, and may we continue to dwell and shine in this unquenchable light of God forever and ever. Amen.

BENEDICTION

———————❧———————

The essence of love is what we do to others both publicly and privately. "And just as you want men to do to you, you also do to them likewise" (Lk.6:31). Love is the inner beauty of our souls and how we come across and interact every day with others. Beloved, may we have more of God's characters every day in us to draw the world to Him; otherwise, how else can we draw them. "Can the blind lead the blind? Will they not both fall into the ditch?" (Lk.6:39).

All our prayers every day for the world should be love. All our prayers every day for the world should be about peace and harmony. All our prayers every day for the world should express kindness and extend words of encouragement to everyone who comes our way. All our prayers for the world should lift, build up, and not tear apart, divide, and conquer every day. May God continue to bless us with this unconditional love that brings peace, unity, and harmony to the world. Beloved, God is a good God. He is love, and do not let anyone preach and fill your hearts with hate, discrimination, and racism. Love your neighbor as yourself (Mk.12:31). Keep your heart pure and your hands clean every day. That is the only way you can walk daily and be rest assured of this eternal hope in God.

Thank you so much for reading. I pray that this book has blessed you just as it has for me. Let us continue to walk in the footsteps of Christ daily and holding onto His commandments. Love fulfills the law of God and sustains us daily in our spiritual journey. We must learn to walk in love and forgive those that have offended us. I see love as the brain, and without it, death occurs. Love is straightforward when we understand the love that the Son of God has shown to us, and there is no greater love than this (Jn.15:13).

We must continue to perfect our walk, and I pray for grace that brings complete transformation and perfection in our lives for you all. "Let love be without hypocrisy. Abhor what is evil, Cling to what is good"(Rm.12:9). Do not let hate enter your heart. Love without hesitation. Mercy keeps us, and we must show that to all instead of condemnation and judgment. I love you all with the love of Christ Jesus, and when you keep on keeping on, nothing can stop you in this journey, and peace becomes your friend in Christ. Stay blessed. Amen.

To request a free copy of this book, write to
Good Shepherd Holy Spirit Ministries
P.O.BOX 593
Nazareth, PA 18064 USA

About Kharis Publishing:

Kharis Publishing, an imprint of Kharis Media LLC, is a leading Christian and inspirational book publisher based in Aurora, Chicago metropolitan area, Illinois. Kharis' dual mission is to give voice to under-represented writers (including women and first-time authors) and equip orphans in developing countries with literacy tools. That is why, for each book sold, the publisher channels some of the proceeds into providing books and computers for orphanages in developing countries, so that these kids may learn to read, dream, and grow. For a limited time, Kharis Publishing is accepting unsolicited queries for nonfiction (Christian, self-help, memoirs, business, health and wellness) from qualified leaders, professionals, pastors, and ministers. Learn more at: About Us - Kharis Publishing - Accepting Manuscript

www.ingramcontent.com/pod-product-compliance
Lightning Source LLC
La Vergne TN
LVHW051605080426
835510LV00020B/3134